SPOT THE LATEST FACEBOOK SCAMS:
STAY SAFE, DON'T BE HIS NEXT VICTIM!

SPOT AND AVOID THE LATEST FACEBOOK SCAMS

SAVE YOURSELF FROM BECOMING THE NEXT VICTIM

LAYOUT BY DANO JANOWSKI
ISBN: 9798344281803

Introduction

What Are the Biggest Scams Happening on Facebook?

Social media has become a hotbed of scams and imposters and among all social networks, Facebook is the top offender.
Over half of its users encounter scams on a weekly basis. No other platform sees such a relentless barrage of fraudulent schemes, making Facebook the top place for cybercriminals to prey on unsuspecting users. In just the first half of 2024 the Federal Trade Commission (FTC) reported that Americans suffered over $1.3 billion in financial losses from digital fraud. Social media platforms alone accounted for a staggering $892 million of that total, with another $461 million lost through websites and apps. These shocking figures represent only the fraud reports submitted to the FTC, which means the true impact for those six months is even greater. The digital world is becoming increasingly dangerous, on Facebook, and these numbers highlight the urgent need for wisdom, vigilance and protection.

Out of all social networks, Facebook has the biggest fraud problem.

This makes it a prime target for cybercriminals. With over 2.9 billion active users, the platform's vast audience provides scammers with endless opportunities to exploit unsuspecting individuals. In fact, more than half of Facebook users have encountered some form of scam on a weekly basis. These scams come in many forms, ranging from fake accounts that impersonate real people or businesses to fraudulent Marketplace listings that trick buyers into paying for non-existent products. Additionally, scammers frequently run deceptive giveaways or contests, luring participants in with promises of large prizes in exchange for personal information.

Cybercriminals are constantly refining their tactics,
making it increasingly difficult for even the most cautious users to detect a scam. The platform's interconnected nature, where users can easily share personal details, interact with friends, and engage in group discussions, offers scammers multiple entry points to carry out their malicious activities.

Table of Contents

In this comprehensive guide, we'll delve into the latest and most common Facebook scams, giving you the tools to recognize suspicious behavior and protect yourself from falling victim.

We'll dive into identifying key red flags, such as fake profiles, suspicious Marketplace offers, and unusual friend requests, while also breaking down how scammers operate on the platform. You'll learn how scammers use tactics like phishing links, fake giveaways, and impersonation schemes to trick users into giving up their personal information or money. We'll explore specific strategies for recognizing if you're interacting with a scammer, such as checking for signs like poor grammar, unrealistic promises, or incomplete profiles.

More importantly, you'll discover practical steps to protect your identity and secure your accounts, such as enabling two-factor authentication, creating strong passwords, and being cautious of unsolicited messages or offers. By understanding how these schemes work, you'll be better equipped to take preventative actions, ensuring your Facebook experience remains safe. With this knowledge, you'll confidently navigate Facebook and shield your personal information from online fraudsters looking to exploit unsuspecting users.

Scammers are constantly developing new techniques to trick users into giving up sensitive data, such as login credentials, personal details, or even financial information.

From phishing links and fake friend requests to fraudulent ads and cloned accounts, these criminals use a variety of deceptive methods to infiltrate your accounts or lure you into costly schemes. Whether it's through convincing charity scams, too-good-to-be-true giveaways, or malicious links hidden in messages that seem legitimate, the threat is very real, and no one is immune.

By understanding the strategies used by scammers, you can take proactive steps to protect yourself

and your loved ones from falling victim to their schemes. Educating yourself on the latest scams circulating across Meta platforms and learning how to recognize red flags is the first line of defense in maintaining your online security and safeguarding your personal information.

Here are the most popular Facebook scams you need to know about:

---

1. Fake prizes and giveaways

Social media scams often involve something "free"
- like apprize, giveaway, or gift card.
- In one common scam, fraudsters create a fake Facebook page for a familiar company,
state lottery, or sweepstakes, and either post offers for free prizes or send victims direct Facebook messages (DMs) claiming they've won.

For example, scammers impersonated Mr. Beast - a very popular YouTuber with over two million followers - & ran Facebook ads claiming you would get $1,000.

Scammers impersonate celebrities on Facebook to make their scam giveaways seem legitimate. But if you respond, you'll be asked to provide personal data to "claim" your prize, such as your credit card numbers or banking details. You may even be pressured into paying fake fees or taxes before you can claim your prize.

Avoid fake giveaway scams on Facebook:

Check the giveaway's Facebook page. When participating in online giveaways, it's crucial to thoroughly check the associated Facebook page. Many lottery scams are cleverly posted on profiles that impersonate official state lottery companies or create fake pages for well-known brands. Fraudulent accounts often show telltale signs, such as a low follower count, indicating a lack of genuine engagement. Additionally, these pages typically have poor-quality designs with amateur graphics and unprofessional layouts. Their posts may contain nonsensical content, typos, and grammatical errors, revealing that they are not maintained by reputable organizations. By scrutinizing these aspects, you can better protect yourself from falling victim to scams.

Don't trust brand names - even if they're verified.

It's essential to remain vigilant and not automatically trust brand names, even when they appear to be verified on social media. Some fraudsters cleverly utilize the names of well-known companies to deceive individuals into thinking they are participating in a legitimate giveaway. For instance, you might come across promotions that claim to be "Costco Customer Appreciation Giveaways," which can easily mislead unsuspecting users. To ensure the giveaway's authenticity, only engage with promotions that are hosted on the company's official brand page. If you encounter a giveaway that seems suspicious or is hosted on a page that isn't the official one, take the extra step to reach out to the company through its official customer support channels. Ask for verification of the giveaway's legitimacy; this diligence can help you avoid falling for a scam.

You're asked to pay an upfront fee to receive your prize.

Be extremely cautious if you encounter any giveaway that requests an upfront fee in order to receive your prize. Scammers often employ this tactic, asking for payments to cover supposed processing fees, taxes, or shipping costs. It's important to remember that legitimate giveaways do not require winners to pay anything upfront. Any request for payment is a clear warning sign of a scam. Real prizes are offered at no cost to the winner, so if you find yourself being asked to pay to claim a prize, it's best to disengage immediately. Protect yourself by recognizing this red flag and steering clear of any promotions that involve financial obligations.

---

2. Charity scams and fraudulent GoFundMe campaigns

Many people have honest intentions to help victims natural disasters.
Unfortunately there are criminals who exploit this altruism as an opportunity for financial gain. These charity scams on platforms like Facebook prey on our natural desire to assist those in need, taking advantage of the compassion that arises during times of crisis. Scammers are often quick to set up fake campaigns, creating duplicate websites and fraudulent GoFundMe pages that are designed to closely mimic legitimate charitable causes.

Charity scams on Facebook prey on our natural desire to help others.

Scammers often create duplicate websites and fraudulent GoFundMe campaigns designed to mimic legitimate causes, tricking unsuspecting individuals into making donations. These fake sites and fundraisers appear convincing, using familiar logos, images, and stories to lure people in. Once a donation is made, the money goes directly to the scammer, leaving victims out of pocket and diverting funds from the real causes that need support.

Avoid fake charity campaigns:

Verify the organization.

Before you donate to any cause, it's crucial to ensure that the charity or organization you're supporting is legitimate. With so many fraudulent campaigns circulating online, taking the time to verify the organization can save you from falling victim to a scam. Start by checking the charity's credentials through trusted sources like the Better Business Bureau's (BBB) website or the Wise Giving Alliance. These organizations provide detailed information on whether a charity meets standards of accountability and transparency. Additionally, websites like CharityNavigator.org can give you insights into the financial health, mission, and effectiveness of the charity. It's also helpful to do a simple Google search, typing in the name of the charity along with terms like "scam," "complaints," or "reviews." This will allow you to see what other people are saying about the organization and whether there are any red flags to be aware of.

Research the organizers.

While online platforms like GoFundMe have made it easier than ever to support personal causes and charities, the ease of creating a fundraising campaign also opens the door for fraudsters to exploit the system. Before donating to any campaign, it's essential to research the organizers behind it. Anyone can create a GoFundMe, so it's important to verify that the person or group raising the money is credible. To do this, search for the charity's name, or the name of the organizer, along with keywords like "complaints," "reviews," "ratings," or "scam." This will help you identify if there have been any past issues or negative feedback. If possible, look for any official affiliations the organizer might have with a reputable charity or check their history of previous campaigns to see if they've delivered on their promises in the past.

Avoid non-traditional payment methods.
One of the biggest red flags in charity scams is the insistence on using non-traditional payment methods. Fraudsters often push for payments through cryptocurrency, gift cards, or peer-to-peer payment apps like Venmo, Zelle, or Carhop because these methods are difficult to trace and nearly impossible to recover if the transaction turns out to be fraudulent. Legitimate charities will never pressure you into using these types of payments and will typically provide multiple secure payment options, such as credit cards, checks, or through well-known platforms like PayPal. If a charity insists on using a non-traditional payment method, it's a strong indicator that something may be wrong. Protect yourself by sticking to recognized and secure payment options, which will offer more recourse if you find yourself dealing with a scam.

---

3. "I can't believe he's gone" posts

One of the Facebook scams starts with a post that reads:
"I can't believe he's gone" or "I'll miss him so much." The post includes a video and is made to look like someone you know has passed away.

The primary goal of these scams is to deceive individuals into clicking on a seemingly innocent video link.

These ultimately redirects them to a counterfeit Facebook login page. This fake page is crafted to look nearly identical to the real Facebook site, making it difficult for users to recognize the deception. If you inadvertently fall for this trick and enter your username and password on the fraudulent page, you will be sharing your login credentials with the scammers behind the operation. Once they have access to your account, they can take control of it, potentially using it for malicious purposes such as spreading further scams, stealing personal information, or even engaging in identity theft.

Avoid fake "He's Gone" scams:

Never click without reading.

It's essential to resist the urge to click on a post, especially when it appears to contain shocking or emotional news. If you see a post with a sensational headline or a vague statement about someone's death, take a moment to fully read the content before you decide to engage.

These posts are often engineered to lead you to dangerous websites.
By simply clicking on the link, it could redirect you to a bogus page that looks like a legitimate news site or social media platform. Even worse, clicking on such links can cause malicious software to be downloaded onto your device without your knowledge, compromising your security and personal information. To protect yourself, always pause and evaluate the post before taking any action.

Look for vague language and dramatic details.
Posts that are part of the "He's Gone" scam often use vague language and exaggerated details to draw you in. They mention a tragedy, using phrases like "tragic news" or "heartbreaking loss," without offering concrete information such as the victim's name or clear details of the event. This vague approach builds curiosity, tempting you to click through for answers. If a post is overly dramatic or lacks specific facts, it's likely part of a scam. Legitimate news sources always provide clear details upfront, including the individual's name and context of the event.

Inspect the link.

Before you click on any link in a suspicious post, take a moment to inspect it thoroughly. You can do this by hovering your mouse cursor over the link, which should reveal the full URL at the bottom of your browser. If the link is obscured, shortened, or redirects to a site that looks unfamiliar or untrustworthy, it's almost certainly a scam. Scammers often use fake URLs or misleading links to trick you into visiting a malicious website that could steal your personal information or infect your device with malware. If the URL looks suspicious, avoid clicking at all costs. However, if you do happen to click, make sure you never share any personal or sensitive information on the next page. Scammers will often prompt you to log in or provide contact details—don't fall for it. Always close the page immediately and consider reporting the scam to the platform where you found it.

It's always wiser to err on the side of caution.

By following these precautions and remaining vigilant, you can steer clear of these emotionally manipulative scams and keep your personal data and devices safe. Remember, it's always better to be cautious and take a moment to think before you click.

4. Marketplace buyers requesting Google Voice codes

Almost one in five users of Facebook Marketplace got scammed recently - both buyers and sellers.

One common Facebook Marketplace scam targeting sellers involves a buyer claiming they need to send a verification code to confirm you're a "real" seller. The scam unfolds when a buyer shows interest in your item and insists on sending a code via text, under the pretense of safety or legitimacy. While this may seem harmless, it's a red flag and a tactic scammers use to exploit your information.

In reality, the scammer is trying to hijack your phone number.

They can do this by linking it to a new account or service, using the code they trick you into sharing. This method allows them to gain unauthorized access to personal accounts, including social media, email, or even financial services, potentially leading to identity theft or fraud. Once the scammer has your phone number and the verification code, they can proceed to use it for malicious purposes, all while you're left unaware of what's happening behind the scenes.

This scam is particularly dangerous because it plays on trust and the seller's desire.

The lister on Marketplace wants to make sure the transaction goes as smooth as possible. Sellers may not think twice before sharing the code, especially when the buyer appears genuinely interested in purchasing the item. To protect yourself, never share any codes or personal information, and insist on using the secure communication features provided by Facebook Marketplace. Scammers frequently try to move conversations off-platform, but staying within the platform's messaging system adds an extra layer of protection.

Example of a Facebook Marketplace scammer asking for a "code" to verify seller's identity.

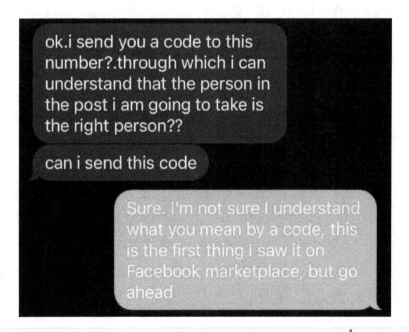

In this scam, someone contacts you about an item for sale and asks for your phone number. The buyer may claim they need to send a verification code to your phone to verify you as a legitimate seller. In reality, the scammer is trying to gain control of your phone number using the code. To avoid this, remember that legitimate buyers will never ask for a verification code. If a buyer requests one, it should raise immediate concern. No transaction should require this step, and you should never share verification codes or personal information with strangers online.

Avoid fraudulent buyers on Facebook Marketplace:

Never send two-factor authentication (2FA) codes or sensitive details to strangers. Don't give it away via any method ever. This information can easily be exploited if it falls into the wrong hands, potentially leading to identity theft or unauthorized access to your accounts. If someone contacts you about an item you're selling, it's essential to prioritize your safety by opting for secure payment methods. The safest options are cash or in-person transactions at a well-lit, public location, such as a coffee shop or busy shopping area.

Ignore requests to move conversations off of Facebook Messenger.

Marketplace Scammers often try to move communications to other platforms, like Discord or email, because once the conversation leaves Facebook, the platform won't be able to monitor the interaction or assist in recovering lost money.

Never accept overpayment (extra money) or checks.

Scam buyers may offer to pay by check or send more money than required, asking you to "refund" the difference. In either case, their payment will likely bounce, leaving you responsible for the deficit and possibly in debt to your bank.

---

5. Underpriced luxury or in-demand items on Marketplace

Another Facebook Marketplace scam involves fraudsters posing as sellers.

Some may post in-demand or luxury items at low prices to get your attention. These sellers almost always have a sob story to explain why they're selling the item so cheaply - for example, to pay for a pet's vet bill or because they're in the military and have been dispatched overseas.

However, when you go to pay, the seller requests a deposit to "hold" the item.

The seller may request a deposit to "hold" the item or may try to pressure you into paying for items via non-eversible methods, such as Zelle or Venmo.

Avoid scam buyers on Facebook Marketplace:

Don't trust deals that are too good to be true.

There are definitely deals to be found on Facebook Marketplace, but if a price seems too cheap to be true, it's a significant warning sign of a potential scam.

Always meet in person (in a safe space) for online transactions.

If a seller is unwilling to meet face-to-face for the exchange, it's a strong indication that they may be trying to scam you. Opt for a safe and secure location like a shopping center, etc. If possible, bring a friend for added safety and support.

If the buying process becomes too complicated - walk away.

Scammers often try to normalize odd scenarios, like claiming a courier will pick up cash and ship the item. If the situation feels too complex or raises red flags, it's likely a scam.

6. Sending "deposits" for items on Marketplace

A recent Marketplace scam involves buyers offering to send a deposit to hold an item.
At first glance, this might seem like a legitimate request, as many sellers might appreciate the assurance of a deposit to secure a sale. However, if you accept the offer, the buyer will then send you what appears to be a legitimate link, instructing you to "deposit" your money at your financial institution. Once you enter your financial information on this fraudulent site, it goes directly to the scammers, who can then use your details to access your bank account and potentially drain your funds.

Many people may not realize they're being scammed until it's too late.
When they find themselves victims of identity theft or financial loss. It's crucial to remember that legitimate buyers will never ask you to send a deposit through a link or website.

Avoid the deposit scam on Facebook Marketplace:

Don't trust links sent from strangers.

Almost all phishing scams involve malicious links. If someone sends you a link - especially to enter financial information - be cautious.

Always double-check the URL before entering information.

Scammers often design fake websites that closely resemble your bank's login page, hoping to trick you into entering your personal information. To protect yourself, always double-check that you're on your bank's official and secure website before entering any account details, passwords, or personal information. Look for signs like a secure connection (https) and verify the website's URL to ensure you're not being redirected to a fraudulent site.

Use a password manager or Safe Browsing tools.

For complete protection, consider using Safe Browsing tools to alert you to fake or malicious websites. Additionally, a reliable password manager can enhance your safety by storing and managing your passwords, ensuring it won't automatically enter your credentials on suspicious or fraudulent sites.

7. Too-good-to-be-true investments (cryptocurrencies, etc.)

Investment fraud almost always end with huge losses for victims.

Investment fraud happens when con artists persuade people to invest in seemingly lucrative opportunities, promising quick, significant returns with little risk. They use deceptive tactics to create urgency, tricking victims into schemes like stocks, cryptocurrency, or real estate. Fraudsters may pose as professionals or use fake testimonials to build trust. Always research thoroughly and be cautious of investments that sound too good to be true.

Scammers often promise impressive returns for just a small initial investment.

Ultimately, it's the fraudsters who profit, often vanishing with their investors' entire savings. Initially, the scammers often paint a picture of success, showcasing testimonials and fabricated evidence of previous investors reaping incredible rewards. This manipulation preys on individuals' hopes and dreams of financial security, luring them into a false sense of confidence.

Once victims hand over their money, they quickly discover promised returns are a ruse.
The fraudsters, who expertly craft elaborate schemes, manipulate investors with convincing pitches and false promises of wealth. These scams are designed to gradually siphon funds from unsuspecting victims, often leading them to invest more over time, believing they're on the verge of a big payoff. However, once the fraudsters have collected enough money, they vanish, taking all the investors' savings with them. These criminals often cover their tracks so well that it becomes nearly impossible to recover the lost funds or trace their whereabouts.

Many victims find themselves not only financially devastated but emotionally scarred by the experience.
The aftermath of such scams can lead to feelings of betrayal, shame, and anger, as individuals grapple with the realization that they have been deceived. Additionally, some victims may even become hesitant to invest in legitimate opportunities in the future, fearing they might fall prey to another scam.

In essence, the only individuals who profit from these deceptive schemes are the fraudsters themselves.

They thrive on the naivety and trust of their victims. It's a sobering reminder of the importance of conducting thorough research and exercising caution when considering any investment opportunity, especially those that seem too good to be true.

Avoid fake investment scams on Facebook:

Ignore claims of "guaranteed" returns.

It's essential to understand that there are no guaranteed investments, particularly when it comes to volatile assets like Bitcoin and other cryptocurrencies. These markets are notoriously unpredictable, and while some may experience sudden surges in value, others can plummet just as quickly. Every investment carries inherent risks, so it's crucial not to be swayed by hype surrounding high returns that seem too good to be true. Remember, if it sounds too easy or effortless, it likely is.

Beware of strange offers from friends and followers.

Be cautious of unusual investment offers from friends and followers. If someone in your network sends unsolicited messages about investing in cryptocurrencies or other ventures, their account may have been compromised. Scammers often hack personal accounts to trick others into investing in fraudulent schemes. To verify the legitimacy of such messages, contact the person through a different method—like a phone call or in-person conversation—to ensure they control their profile and genuinely endorse the investment opportunity.

It's crucial to do your due diligence and conduct thorough research.

Before committing to any investment, take the time to research thoroughly. The most successful investors study companies, analyze market trends, and understand the risks involved. Familiarizing yourself with how the market works and staying updated with relevant news can help you make informed decisions. Without this effort, investing can feel like gambling with your savings. In the world of investments, knowledge is power and it can protect you from scams while increasing your chances of real financial growth.

8. Romance and sextortion scams

Most romance scams occur entirely online, where new relationships lead to requests for money.
Scammers often take their time to build a rapport with their targets, leveraging platforms like Facebook to create an illusion of intimacy and connection. Once they gain the trust of their victims, these fraudsters employ tactics of social engineering & emotional manipulation, skillfully persuading their targets to send money under various pretenses - whether it's for a supposed emergency, travel expenses, or medical bills.

Sextortion, a dark twist on romance scams.
In these cases, imposters convince their targets to share explicit photos or videos, often under the guise of a romantic relationship. Once the victim complies, the fraudsters immediately demand payment, threatening to release the explicit materials to the victim's friends and family if they refuse. This form of manipulation can leave individuals feeling trapped, ashamed, and desperate, as the fear of public humiliation can compel them to comply with the scammers' demands.

How to identify and avoid these Facebook scams:

Beware of excessive flattery.

If your new online relationship is moving unusually fast or if the other person is showering you with compliments and attention, consider these major red flags. Scammers often try to accelerate the relationship to create a sense of urgency, pressuring you to make hasty decisions about money. They aim to exploit your emotions while you're caught up in the excitement of what feels like a blossoming romance. Be cautious of anyone who rushes intimacy or brings up financial issues too soon.

Tighten your privacy practices.

Facebook scams thrive on the vast personal information available on social media. To protect yourself, be mindful of what you share publicly— especially sensitive details like your phone number and home address. Scammers often use this information to impersonate you or target you with personalized fraud. Adjust your privacy settings so that only trusted friends can access your details, making it harder for scammers to gather intel. Regularly reviewing these settings is a good habit to ensure ongoing protection..

End contact with suspicious individuals.

If you encounter a new Facebook friend with minimal information posted on their profile or who refuses to engage in a video chat to verify their identity, it's crucial to scrutinize their genuine intentions carefully. Profiles that lack detail or seem incomplete can be significant red flags, indicating that the account may not be legitimate. Scammers often create fake accounts with little to no information to lure unsuspecting users into a false sense of security. Additionally, if someone is hesitant or outright refuses to engage in a video chat, it could suggest they are hiding something or are not who they claim to be, which should raise further suspicions.

In such situations, the safest course of action is to terminate all contact and block them from your online networks to prevent any potential threats to your personal safety and security. Trusting your instincts is vital; if something feels off or too good to be true, it's always wiser to take a cautious approach. Remember, it's better to err on the side of caution than to risk exposing yourself to potential scams or fraudulent activities.

9. Hacked or cloned friend accounts asking for 2FA codes

Two-factor authentication (2FA) codes serve as a crucial additional layer of security.

Two-factor authentication (2FA) is designed to protect your online accounts and keep hackers at bay by adding an extra layer of security. These codes help verify your identity, ensuring that only you are able to access your account, making unauthorized access far less likely. However, scammers have become more sophisticated in their tactics and are finding ways to trick people into unknowingly sharing their 2FA codes. One common method involves scammers using a cloned account that appears to be someone you trust, like a close friend or family member. The scammer will message you, claiming that they accidentally sent their 2FA code to your phone number or email by mistake, asking you to forward it to them. In reality, the code is for your account, and by sharing it, you give the scammer access to your private information. Always be wary of such requests, even from people you know, and double-check their identity before sharing any sensitive information.

Example of a scammer trying to trick a Facebook user into sharing a 2FA code.

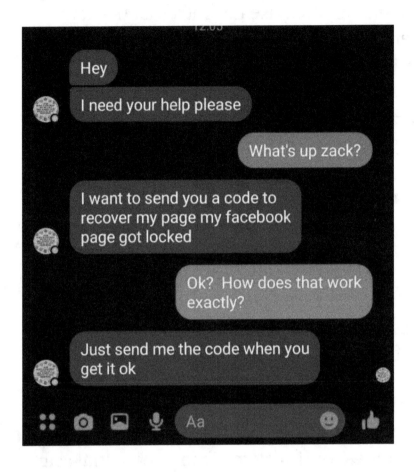

Avoid getting scammed by a hacked or cloned account:

Never share 2FA codes.

If anyone asks you to send them your two-factor authentication (2FA) code, proceed with caution—it's highly likely that they're a scammer.

Legitimate individuals or companies will never ask for your 2FA code or one-time passwords. Scammers often use deceptive tactics to manipulate people into believing that they need access to these codes for various reasons, such as troubleshooting an issue, verifying your account, or even assisting you with a supposed problem they claim to be experiencing.

Contact the person.

If you receive a suspicious message requesting your two-factor authentication (2FA) codes, it's crucial to take immediate action to protect your account. Instead of responding directly to the message, reach out to the person through a different communication platform, such as a phone call, text message, or a direct message on a social media app you know is secure. This extra step allows you to verify whether the request is legitimate or if it stems from a potential scammer impersonating them. Be cautious and ensure you have their correct contact information before reaching out, as scammers may use fake accounts that mimic those of your friends or family. By confirming the authenticity of the request through an independent channel, you can better safeguard your personal information and avoid falling victim to scams that exploit trust and urgency.

Change your account passwords.

If you receive an email about a two-factor authentication (2FA) request that you did not initiate, it's a clear warning sign that someone may be trying to gain unauthorized access to your account. In such situations, it's crucial to act quickly to protect your personal information and secure your online presence. Begin by immediately updating your password, making sure it is both unique and complex.

A strong password should be a mix of uppercase and lowercase letters, numbers, and special characters.

This reduces the risk of it being guessed or cracked. In addition to updating your password, consider enabling any additional security features your account offers, such as receiving notifications for suspicious or unusual login attempts. You can also opt for stronger authentication methods, like biometric verification or hardware-based security keys, which further reduce the likelihood of unauthorized access. Staying vigilant and using these proactive measures can significantly enhance the security of your accounts.

10. *"Is this you?" video link scams*

One of the older Facebook scams that continues to circulate

This scam involves receiving a message from someone in your network, often with a video link and a question like, "Is this you?" to spark curiosity. It plays on the trust within your social circle, making you more likely to click without hesitation. The sender appears genuine, using a familiar name and profile picture, lowering your guard and increasing your vulnerability to the scam.

However, clicking on the provided link can lead to a fraudulent website.

These are aimed at stealing your information or downloading malicious software onto your device. Engaging with such content not only puts your Facebook account at risk but also jeopardizes your personal identifiable information (PII), which can include sensitive data like your email address, phone number, and financial details. To protect yourself, avoid clicking on suspicious links, and verify the legitimacy of any unusual messages before taking action.

Avoid these Facebook scams:

Ignoring suspicious messages is crucial in protecting your online security.
It's essential to resist the temptation to click on links or videos included in these messages, as doing so can lead to potential threats. Instead, take proactive steps by deleting the message immediately. This action will help ensure that you don't accidentally click on it later, which could compromise your account or device. Staying vigilant in this way is a key strategy in safeguarding your personal information from malicious actors who use deceptive tactics to gain access to your accounts.

Flagging the issue is an important next step.
Scam messages often come from hacked profiles of real friends. To address this, contact your friend through another method to let them know, so they can secure their account. Also, report the scam to Facebook to help protect others and combat online fraud. By staying proactive, you can play a role in keeping your network safer from these kinds of threats.

Utilizing Safe Browsing tools.

This is a highly effective way to boost your digital security and add an extra layer of protection when navigating the internet. These tools work by automatically detecting and blocking scam messages, phishing attempts, and malicious websites, notifying you whenever you're about to engage with suspicious content. This proactive defense helps you avoid accidentally clicking harmful links or entering unsafe websites, which could compromise your personal data or infect your device with malware. By incorporating Safe Browsing tools into your daily online activities, you create a safer browsing experience and significantly reduce the risk of falling victim to scams.

In addition to employing Safe Browsing tools, maintaining a mindset of vigilance is crucial. Regularly reviewing your privacy settings, staying aware of the latest scams, and being cautious about the information you share online all contribute to staying protected. Reporting any suspicious activity to platforms like Facebook not only helps you but also safeguards others from falling into similar traps. By actively participating in this process, you become part of a broader effort to combat online fraud and maintain a safer digital space for everyone.

11. Facebook quiz scams

You may think taking a Facebook quiz is fun.
If you notice, many of the questions are actually common cybersecurity questions. For example, the quiz may ask you to share your name, date of birth, mother's maiden name, pet's name, email address, or phone number. With your guard down, you may unknowingly disclose sensitive information that compromises your online security.

Avoid falling victim to Facebook quiz scams:

Stick to reputable companies.
If you want to take a quiz on Facebook, only engage on trusted pages that provide a lot of reviews and proof of legitimacy. For example, Unilad or Buzzfeed would be safer than a random page that you see for the first time.

Use unique password recovery questions.
Although quizzes may include common security questions, using unique questions and answers for your online accounts is wise. That way, nobody can access your account if they know your mother's maiden name.

12. Offers of "free money" from government programs

In this scam, you receive a direct message (DM) from someone you know on Facebook. Some claim the government is offering grants for various purposes. The message may include enticing details, such as your friend sharing their experience of receiving thousands of dollars for tragedy relief. While this may seem like an incredible opportunity, it's crucial to approach such messages with caution. If a scammer has hacked your friend's account, they could be using it to spread misinformation and lure you into a trap. Engaging with their message might compromise your personal information or lead to financial losses.

Remember that legitimate government grants typically require thorough application processes.
They do not use social media to send these messages. Therefore, before responding to any such offers, verify the information independently and confirm the authenticity of the message to protect yourself from becoming the next victim in this insidious scam.

Avoid these Facebook scams:

Ignore messages about government grants.
The government doesn't contact people on Facebook to give away free money; any message you receive about this is a scam.

Research government grants on official websites.
If you need financial assistance, it's important to research legitimate government programs on your own. Look for official websites ending in ".gov" and make sure they use "HTTPS" for a secure connection. You can also contact government agencies directly through verified phone numbers or local offices to get accurate information. This approach helps you avoid scams and ensures you're accessing genuine support.

Report these Facebook scams.
You should notify Facebook about spam messages or compromised accounts as soon as possible to prevent others from becoming victims. Reporting these incidents not only helps protect your immediate circle but also contributes to the overall safety of the platform. By acting quickly, you help Facebook address the issue promptly and remove potential threats before further harm.

13. Ads for phony items or fake e-commerce sites

Nearly 70% of all online shopping scams originate on platforms like Facebook and Instagram.
Cybercrooks are capitalizing on the vast audience these social media sites provide. In most cases, the scam begins with a fake advertisement that tempts potential victims with seemingly irresistible low-cost items. However, if you click on the ad, you'll likely be redirected to a fraudulent website designed to steal your payment details, or you may find yourself paying for a counterfeit or low-quality product that never arrives. The allure of getting a great deal can cloud judgment, making it crucial to remain vigilant when encountering unfamiliar sellers online.

To help you spot fake e-commerce sites on Facebook, be on the lookout for several red flags.
One of the most telling signs is extremely cheap or even free products, as scammers often use these bait prices to lure victims in, sometimes claiming that you only need to cover shipping costs. As a rule of thumb, if a deal seems too good to be true, it probably is.

Additionally, be wary of requests for payment via gift cards;

legitimate sellers will typically offer secure payment options like Meta Pay (formerly Facebook Pay), which provides purchase protection. Another indicator of a scam is a suspicious e-commerce website that appears poorly designed, contains spelling errors, or lacks proper functionality.

Finally, while a bogus site may showcase reviews, these are often fabricated.

To verify a store's reputation, start with a Google search of the company name to uncover insights into their business practices, customer experiences, and any potential red flags. Explore beyond the first few results for a more comprehensive understanding of the seller's history. Additionally, check reviews on trusted third-party sites like Trustpilot, where you can find honest feedback from actual customers about their experiences, product quality, and customer service reliability. Pay attention to the overall rating and recurring themes in the reviews—both positive and negative—to assess the seller's credibility. By doing thorough research, you can ensure you're dealing with a trustworthy seller before making any purchases.

14. Phishing emails or messages from Facebook's team

Fraudsters impersonate Facebook's support. Fraudsters often impersonate Facebook's support team through phishing emails designed to steal your login information or allow the perpetrators to sneak malware onto your device. These deceptive communications can take various forms, making them difficult to identify.

One common scam involves messages that warn users their "account is being disabled." These often create a sense of urgency that pressures individuals to act quickly. In another variation, you may receive direct messages from a page labeled "Facebook Security Monitor" claiming that your account has been breached, that your payment has failed, or that there's something that requires immediate attention. These messages often include links that direct you to fake login pages, where you may unknowingly provide your credentials to the scammers. Always be cautious of unexpected messages and verify the legitimacy of any communication before clicking links or providing personal information.

Example of a fake password reset email claiming to be from Facebook.

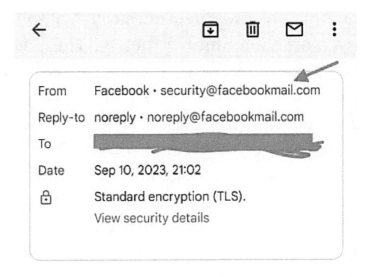

From	Facebook · security@facebookmail.com
Reply-to	noreply · noreply@facebookmail.com
To	
Date	Sep 10, 2023, 21:02
	Standard encryption (TLS). View security details

Hi Paulo,

We received a request to reset your Facebook password.
Enter the following password reset code:

66631625

Alternatively, you can directly change your password.

Change password

If you panic in response to a suspicious message or alert.

You might find yourself instinctively clicking on the link or answering their questions without taking a moment to think critically. This impulsive action can have serious consequences, as it could grant fraudsters easy access to your Facebook account and compromise your personal information. Once they gain access, they can manipulate your account, send messages to your contacts, and potentially use your identity to conduct further scams. It's essential to pause and assess any unexpected requests, verify their authenticity, and approach them cautiously.

Cybercriminals often employ tactics designed to provoke immediate fear or urgency.

They want to entice you to act quickly rather than carefully evaluate the situation. Once they gain access, they can hijack your account, potentially using it to perpetrate further scams on your friends and family or even to gather more of your sensitive information. Therefore, it's crucial to remain calm and composed when faced with unexpected messages, allowing yourself the time to assess the legitimacy of the communication before taking any action that could jeopardize your online security.

How to spot a Facebook phishing scam:

Check the sender's email address.
Click the sender's "From" name to verify the source. Genuine Facebook emails always come from an **@facebook.com** address. Scrutinize the URL before entering your login credentials. Phishing emails usually contain links that direct you to fake Facebook login pages (or download malware onto your device). Hover over the links to see if the URL looks suspicious - for instance, it may include a close variation or strange domain, such as "facebookmail.com", "faceb00k.com" or "Facebook.XYZ."

Look out for urgency.
Scammers often create a false sense of urgency to pressure you into making hasty decisions. They may claim your account is at risk of being banned or deleted immediately unless you take action right away. However, legitimate Facebook emails will never threaten users with instant consequences like this. Always take the time to review such messages carefully, and if something seems suspicious, be skeptical and avoid rushing into any action. Verifying the message directly through official channels is always a safer approach.

15. Work-from-home & other bogus job offers

As more people embrace the "working from home" lifestyle, fake job offers constitute a growing problem.

In 2023, fake business opportunity scams cost on average $6,183 per victim.
According to the Federal Trade Commission (FTC), these deceptive schemes have become a significant financial burden, leaving many in difficult situations. They often promise high returns with minimal effort, luring individuals with the promise of quick wealth. However, behind these enticing offers are fraudsters who manipulate victims into investing their hard-earned money into fake or poorly constructed business ventures.

In the first half of 2024, Americans suffered over $1.3 billion in financial losses from digital fraud.
Social media platforms alone accounted for a staggering $892 million of that total, with another $461 million lost through websites and apps according to reports from the Federal Trade Commission (FTC).

These Facebook scams often start with an enticing job offer.

These draw applicants in by asking for sensitive onboarding information like Social Security numbers (SSNs) and bank account details. Providing this data increases the likelihood that your information will be stolen and sold on the Dark Web.

How to spot a fake job scam:

The perks and salary seem too good to be true.
Scammers dangle high salaries and generous benefits packages to ensnare victims who are desperate to land good jobs. You should verify everything about a company and its typical salary range through a third-party review site, like Glassdoor.

You're asked to pay a fee to apply.
Legitimate employers will never request processing fees or any form of payment during the application process. These scams are designed to exploit job seekers by taking their money without providing any real employment opportunities. If you encounter such a request, it's crucial to end all contact immediately and block the person or entity involved.

They don't want to meet via video calls.

If the prospective employer isn't willing to have a video call with you, consider this a red flag. When you request one, take note if the employer becomes defensive or tries to pressure you by saying they'll move on to the next candidate if you don't accept immediately.

Reminder Steps to Avoid Facebook Scams

With its anonymous nature and over three billion users, Facebook is a breeding ground for scams. To avoid falling victim to social media cybercriminals, it's essential to adopt a vigilant and proactive attitude. Staying alert is key to steering clear of the dangers they present.

Here's a summary to help keep yourself safe on Facebook and other social networking sites:

Use a strong & unique password for your Facebook account.
Complex passwords that combine uppercase and lowercase letters, numbers, and symbols can help reduce the risk of account takeover or fraud. If you're unable to log in, visit facebook.com/help and type "Can't Login" to find directions for recovering your account.

Enable two-factor authentication (2FA).

You can make your accounts more secure by adding a second authentication factor to the login process - like a fingerprint scan, push notification, or hardware security key.

Tighten your online privacy settings.

Adjust your profile visibility and privacy settings to improve your social media security. Securing your profile and removing sensitive information will make you less likely to fall victim to fraud.

Turn on Facebook's login alerts to warn you of hacking.

Login alerts are an important security feature that notify you whenever someone logs into your Facebook account from an unrecognized device, browser, or location. This proactive measure keeps you informed about any suspicious activity and serves as an early warning system for potential unauthorized access. Upon receiving a login alert, you can quickly take action, such as changing your password or reviewing your account settings, to enhance your security. These alerts help you identify if someone has compromised your account, allowing you to respond promptly to safeguard your personal information and maintain your online security.

Check your login and active session history for suspicious activity.

Look for logins from locations you've never visited and actions you don't remember taking (such as liking posts, following new pages, or adding new friends).

Use Facebook's "Security Checkup" tool to update your account privacy.

This tool allows you to thoroughly review and enhance the security measures associated with your Facebook profile. The Security Checkup guides you through various settings and options to help ensure your account remains protected from potential threats. Before you can begin this process, you must log in to your account first. Once logged in, the tool will prompt you to assess your current security settings, including two-factor authentication, password strength, and active sessions. By taking advantage of the Security Checkup, you can add additional layers of protection, helping to safeguard your personal information and maintain your privacy while using the platform. Regularly utilizing this tool is an effective way to stay ahead of evolving security risks on social media.

Never click on suspicious links in Facebook DMs, emails, or texts.

If you receive an unsolicited message with links and little context, it's best not to click. Even if the message appears to be from a friend, it could be the first step in a scam.

Decline friend requests from strangers or duplicates.

Report scammers to Facebook.

Reporting a scam allows Facebook to investigate and take the appropriate action, like reporting them to the proper authorities, removing the scammer's profile or banning their account.

Monitor your identity and credit.

If you think you've encountered any Facebook scams, keep an eye on your bank statements and credit reports for signs of fraud. Even small transactions are worth querying, as fraudsters may test the account by defrauding you with small amounts before draining your savings, checking account, or applying for a credit card in your name.

The Bottom Line: Stay Safe on Social Media.

As social media users, we must be vigilant about the risks of account compromise and fraud. The more people who successfully safeguard their accounts from scammers, the less appealing these scams become to cybercriminals. However, even with caution, you may still fall victim to fraud, as criminals continue to evolve their tactics, especially with the help of Artificial Intelligence (AI).

To further protect yourself, consider using a credit card and identity theft monitoring service to secure your personal information and financial accounts from fraud. You can explore various services by searching online for "credit card and identity theft monitoring services.

Stay secure, stay ahead of the risks!

www.ingramcontent.com/pod-product-compliance
Lightning Source LLC
LaVergne TN
LVHW051750050326
832903LV00029B/2828